LEADING *With* LOVE
Study Guide

About the Author:

Alexander Strauch has served as a teacher and pastor elder at Littleton Bible Chapel in Littleton, Colorado, for more than thirty years. He and his wife, Marilyn, have four children and six grandchildren.

Other books by Alexander Strauch include:

Biblical Eldership:
An Urgent Call to Restore Biblical Church Leadership

The New Testament Deacon:
Minister of Mercy

The Hospitality Commands

Agape Leadership:
Lessons in Spiritual Leadership from the Life of R.C. Chapman
(coauthored with Robert L. Peterson)

Men and Women:
Equal Yet Different

A Christian Leader's Guide to

LEADING *With* LOVE
Study Guide

Alexander Strauch

Lewis & Roth Publishers

Leading with Love: Study Guide
ISBN: 0-93608-322-0
Copyright © 2006 by Alexander Strauch. All rights reserved.

Editor: Amanda Sorenson
Cover Design: Resolution Design

Scripture quotations are from THE HOLY BIBLE, ENGLISH STANDARD VERSION®, copyright © 2001 by Crossway Bibles, a division of Good News Publishers. Used by permission. All rights reserved.

Printed in the United States of America
First Printing 2006

To receive a free catalog of books published by Lewis and Roth Publishers, please call toll free 800-477-3239 or visit our website, *www.lewisandroth.org*.

Lewis and Roth Publishers
P.O. Box 469
Littleton, Colorado 80160

Contents

Introduction

Connecting Love and Leadership

Pursue love....

1 Cor. 14:1

This guide is designed so that Christian leaders and teachers may study with other leaders and teachers the book, *A Christian Leader's Guide to Leading with Love.* If you lead or teach people at any level in the church—as a Sunday school teacher, youth worker, women's or men's ministry leader, Bible study leader, administrator, music director, elder, deacon, pastor, missionary, or evangelist—this study is for you and your colleagues.

Jesus Christ, the master leader and teacher, trained his disciples as a group. Learning to work together in love was paramount to Jesus' training of his disciples. Indeed, he gave them a "new commandment" to love one another as he had loved them. By this community of love, the world would know that they were Christ's disciples (John 13:34-35).

In keeping with Christ's example, Christians learn about love from God's book, the Bible, and from interacting with one another—particularly in the context of the church, the family of God. Christlike love for others cannot be learned merely by reading a book in isolation from people. Math and history can be learned by reading a book, but not love. Love requires a minimum of two persons, the lover and the beloved.

By studying love in leadership in fellowship with other leaders and teachers, you will gain a more accurate understanding of loving leadership. Furthermore, and this is very important, you will create an atmosphere and mind-set among your local church leaders that will

1

continually reinforce the biblical principles of leading with love. As a result, you will help one another to become more loving, Christlike leaders.

A number of questions in this study requires that you explain the meaning of key Scripture passages. I encourage you to use Bible tools and commentaries to help you grasp the meaning of these significant passages. Other questions are designed to make you evaluate your ministry in terms of love and to help you apply the New Testament principles of love to your leadership. All the questions are meant to help you understand the (1) indispensability of love to Christian leadership, (2) the character and behavior of a loving Christian leader, and (3) the works of a loving Christian leader or teacher.

By studying together *Leading with Love*, you will in part fulfill the biblical injunction to "pursue love" (1 Cor. 14:1). But remember, learning to lead with love is a life-long process, not a single study.

Teacher's Guide

If you are leading or facilitating a group study on *Leading with Love*, I highly recommend that you use the *Teacher's Guide*. It will give you the right answers to the questions in the *Study Guide* along with many helpful suggestions for leading the study.

Lesson One

Love Is Indispensable to Christian Leadership

This lesson covers pages 1 to 17 of *Leading with Love*. Read these pages before doing the lesson.

Begin Your Session by Reading the Passages Below

And I will show you a still more excellent way. If I speak in the tongues of men and of angels, but have not love, I am a noisy gong or a clanging cymbal. And if I have prophetic powers, and understand all mysteries and all knowledge, and if I have all faith, so as to remove mountains, but have not love, I am nothing. If I give away all I have, and if I deliver up my body to be burned, but have not love, I gain nothing. (1 Cor. 12:31-13:3)

Let all that you do be done in love. (1 Cor. 16:14)

Above all, keep loving one another earnestly. (1 Peter 4:8)

And above all these put on love, which binds everything together in perfect harmony. (Col. 3:14)

Owe no one anything, except to love each other. (Rom. 13:8)

Anyone who does not love does not know God, because God is love. (1 John 4:8)

3

Connecting Love and Leadership

1. The author lists four reasons for applying the doctrine of love to Christian leadership. Which one of these four reasons do you find most stimulating to your thinking about the connection between love and leadership? Explain your choice.

Chapter 1: Five Minus One Equals Zero

2. As you read D. L. Moody's account of his encounter with the biblical doctrine of love, which two of his statements most challenged your thinking about love? Explain your choices.

3. Apart from Jesus Christ, why is Paul the most important New Testament figure in regard to the Christian doctrine of love and leadership? List as many reasons as you can.

4. Using the verses below, describe Paul's leadership style and character before he was converted to Christ on the road to Damascus (Acts 9:3-9).

- But Saul [Paul] was ravaging the church, and entering house after house, he dragged off men and women and committed them to prison. (Acts 8:3)
- But Saul, still breathing threats and murder against the disciples of the Lord (Acts 9:1)
- And I punished them often in all the synagogues and tried to make them blaspheme, and in raging fury against them I persecuted them even to foreign cities. (Acts 26:11)
- For you have heard of my former life in Judaism, how I persecuted the church of God violently and tried to destroy it. (Gal. 1:13)
- I was a blasphemer, persecutor, and insolent opponent. (1 Tim. 1:13)

5. What do the following verses reveal about Paul's leadership style and character after his conversion to Christ?

Romans 9:1-3

1 Corinthians 16:24

2 Corinthians 1:24

2 Corinthians 2:4

2 Corinthians 6:4, 6

2 Corinthians 7:3

2 Corinthians 12:14-15

Philippians 1:8; 4:1

1 Thessalonians 2:7-8

1 Thessalonians 2:11-12

Reflections

Much work within the local church (and among local churches) is done in group settings: elders' and deacons' meetings, staff meetings, board meetings, committee meetings, and all-church meetings. The longer we work together, the more we get to know one another's faults and annoying personality traits, which can make life together

frustrating. Understanding the New Testament principles of love will significantly enhance healthy group leadership, group meetings, and congregational life as a whole.

Leading with Love, page 2

---

6. In light of what we have seen of Paul's change of character and style of leadership, what change would you like to make in your ministry with people?

7. First Corinthians 13:1-3 is considered to be one of Paul's most skillfully written passages. What is the main point of this literary masterpiece?

8. Scripture teaches that spiritual gifts are divinely bestowed upon believers. According to the following passages, what are God's purposes for giving his people these gifts?

1 Corinthians 12:7, 25

1 Corinthians 14:3, 4, 5, 12, 17, 19, 26, 31

Ephesians 4:11-16

1 Peter 4:10-11

9. In what way(s) did the Corinthians misunderstand God's purpose for spiritual gifts and err in practicing those gifts?

10. As a Christian leader or teacher, how can you protect yourself from repeating the same sins and mistakes that the Corinthians made in regard to the practice of spiritual gifts and one's service to others?

11. List some reasons why "knowledge" without love is dangerous to the local church and the whole body of Christ.

12. Explain how it is possible for a person to give away all his or her possessions to feed the poor and yet fail to make that sacrifice as an act of love. Can you give a biblical example of loveless sacrificial giving?

13. What do you think the Corinthians thought when they first heard Paul's letter read in the congregational meeting? Use your sanctified imagination.

14. How has *Lesson One* on 1 Corinthians 13:1-3 changed your way of thinking about yourself and the ministry God has given to you?

Reflections

Without love, our most extraordinary gifts and highest achievements are ultimately fruitless to the church and before God. In Paul's way of thinking, nothing has lasting, spiritual value unless it springs from love.

Leading with Love, page 16

Lesson Two

Love Is Indispensable to Christian Leadership

This lesson covers pages 19 to 35 of *Leading with Love*. Read these pages before doing the lesson.

Begin Your Session by Reading the Passages Below

I know your works, your toil and your patient endurance, and how you cannot bear with those who are evil, but have tested those who call themselves apostles and are not, and found them to be false.... But I have this against you, that you have abandoned the love you had at first. Remember therefore from where you have fallen; repent, and do the works you did at first. If not, I will come to you and remove your lampstand from its place, unless you repent. (Rev. 2:2, 4-5)

For the love of Christ controls us, because we have concluded this: that one has died for all, therefore all have died; and he died for all, that those who live might no longer live for themselves but for him who for their sake died and was raised. (2 Cor. 5:14-15)

You shall love the Lord your God with all your heart and with all your soul and with all your mind. This is the great and first commandment. And a second is like it: You shall love your neighbor as yourself. On these two commandments depend all the Law and the Prophets. (Matt. 22:37-40)

11

A new commandment I give to you, that you love one another: just as I have loved you, you also are to love one another. By this all people will know that you are my disciples, if you have love for one another. (John 13:34-35)

Chapter 2: Love or Die

1. The church in the city of Ephesus had many commendable qualities. What were these positive qualities (see Rev. 2:1-3, 6)?

2. Despite all its commendable qualities, something was dreadfully wrong in the church at Ephesus. In your own words, clearly describe the problem. Be as specific as possible.

3. **a.** Using biblical terminology, describe the kind of love God requires of his people toward himself.

b. Describe the kind of love God requires among believers toward one another.

c. Describe the kind of love God requires of believers toward unbelievers.

Reflections

Unlove is deadly. It is a cancer. It may kill slowly but it always kills in the end. Let us fear it, fear to give room to it as we should fear to nurse a cobra. It is deadlier than any cobra. And just as one minute drop of the almost invisible cobra venom spreads swiftly all over the body of one into whom it has been injected, so one drop of the gall of unlove in my heart or yours, however unseen, has a terrible power of spreading all through our Family, for we are one body—we are parts of one another....

If unlove be discovered anywhere, stop everything and put it right, if possible at once.

Amy Carmichael

---

4. List the three remedies Jesus prescribes for the loveless church (Rev. 2:5, 7) and explain how a local church could implement each one.

5. How would you answer someone who accused Jesus Christ of not being loving because of his severe threat of judgment on the church at Ephesus? (For help, see Acts 20:28; Heb. 12:5-11; Rev. 3:19.)

6. What kind of responsibilities does Revelation 2:2-6 suggest should be a part of a Christian leader's and teacher's work load?

7. How should the truths of Revelation 2:4-5 profoundly affect a Christian leader's and teacher's personal spiritual life?

Reflections

In a sin-saturated world, repentance and spiritual revitalization are never-ending tasks. So let the leaders and teachers of the church be prepared to lead the congregation in repentance for lovelessness and hypocritical love (Rom. 12:9). Love can be revived and grow afresh (Rev. 2:5). The fire can be rekindled. Lives can be rededicated to Christ and one another. The fresh life of love can be breathed into

prayer, Bible study, evangelism, worship, and fellowship with others. To that end let us continually pray and work.

Leading with Love, page 25

Chapter 3: The Motivating Power of Love

8. In 2 Corinthians 5:14-15, Paul explains the "driving, motivating force of his life:"

> For the love of Christ controls us, because we have concluded this: that one has died for all, therefore all have died; and he died for all, that those who live might no longer live for themselves but for him who for their sake died and was raised.

It is essential that you understand this highly significant passage of Scripture. Give a brief explanation of each of the following key words and clauses. If you can, use a good commentary(s) or any other Bible tools.

a. What does the word *control* (Greek, *synechō*) mean in this context?

b. "For the love of Christ controls us"

c. What does the word *concluded* (Greek, *krinō*) mean in this context? What point is Paul making by means of this key word?

d. "Therefore all have died"

e. "Those who live might no longer live for themselves but for him who for their sakes died and was raised"

9. How would a proper understanding of 2 Corinthians 5:14-15 improve your leadership and teaching ministry?

———————————

Reflections

If Jesus Christ be God and died for me, then no sacrifice can be too great for me to make for Him.

C.T. Studd

———————————

10. In Ephesians 3:17-19, Paul prays to the Father that we might be empowered by the Holy Spirit of God to comprehend the amazing "love of Christ:"

that you...may have strength to comprehend with all the saints what is the breadth and length and height and depth [of Christ's love], and to know the love of Christ that surpasses knowledge.

Why is it essential for you as a Christian leader to understand the amazing love of Christ and to continue probing its depths throughout life?

11. Of the four examples of people who were motivated and transformed by "the love of Christ," which one most touched your heart and mind? Explain why.

12. What are the connections between our leadership ministry and the "great and first commandment" to love God with the totality of our being? List as many answers as you can.

Reflections

We should, of course, seek to continually improve our skills in leadership, personal discipline, time management, interpersonal relationships, and teaching. But above all these things, we should seek to increase our knowledge and enjoyment of Christ and deepen our love for him (Phil 3:8-14).

Leading with Love, page 30

---

13. Below is a list of ways to help develop and maintain *a deeper love relationship with God through Jesus Christ:*

(1) by a personal commitment (with the Holy Spirit's help) to obey "the great and first commandment" to love God unreservedly and to love the Lord Jesus Christ preeminently above all others (Deut. 6:4-5; 13:3; Jos. 23:11; Ps. 27:4; Matt. 10:37; 22:37-38; Mark 12:28-34; Luke 10:25-28; 14:26; John 21:15-17; Phil. 1:21; 3:13-14).

(2) by living in obedience to Christ's commands: "For this is the love of God [love for God], that we keep his commandments" (1 John 5:3).

(3) by not loving the world and its idols: "Do not love the world or the things in the world. If anyone loves the world, the love of the Father [love for the Father] is not in him" (1 John 2:15; also James 4:4).

(4) by loving and serving God's people: "For he who does not love his brother whom he has seen cannot love God whom he has not seen. And this commandment we have from him: whoever loves God must also love his brother" (1 John 4:20-21; also 11-12; James 1:27).

(5) by reading, studying, and meditating on God's Word, the Scriptures, in order to know him as the great God that he is (Deut. 17:18-20). "For consider what great things he has done for you" (1 Sam. 12:24). D. A. Carson doesn't hesitate to say,

> but I doubt that it is possible to obey the first command without reading the Bible a great deal.... How on earth shall we love him with heart and mind if we do not increasingly know him, know what he likes and what he loathes, know what he has disclosed, know what he commands and what he forbids?

(6) by communing regularly with him in prayer: "Be constant in

prayer" (Rom.12:12). This will include confession of sin, praise, and intercession for others.

(7) by worshiping him in song, praise, thanksgiving, and "in remembrance" of his substitutionary death through the elements of the bread and cup (1 Cor. 11:23-32; Rev. 5:9-14).

a. Of these seven ways to deepen your love relationship with God through Christ, which two are the most difficult for you to practice consistently? Explain why.

b. Of these seven ways to deepen your love relationship with God through Christ, which two help you most to maintain your relationship with Christ? Explain.

c. Of these seven ways to deepen your love relationship with God through Christ, which one needs your immediate attention? Describe several steps you can take to improve.

Reflections

If I allow my work to get between my heart and the Master, it will be little worth. We can only effectually serve Christ as we are enjoying Him. It is while the heart dwells upon His powerful attractions that the hands perform the most acceptable service to His name…. The man who will present Christ to others must be occupied with Christ for himself.

C. H. Mackintosh

---

14. It is important to your leadership ministry that you understand the "new commandment" of John 13:34-35:

> A new commandment I give to you, that you love one another: just as I have loved you, you also are to love one another. By this all people will know that you are my disciples, if you have love for one another.

a. In light of the Old Testament commandments to love God and neighbor (Deut. 6:4-5; Lev. 19:18), what is "new" about the "new commandment" of Jesus?

b. What are the chief characteristics of a leadership style patterned after the "new commandment" (John 13:34; see also 1 John 3:16; Eph. 5:2, 26)?

15. The verses below express Paul's self-sacrificing love for his converts. Read them carefully and prayerfully.

♦ I hold you in my heart.... For God is my witness, how I yearn for you all with the affection of Christ Jesus. (Phil. 1:7-8)

♦ Therefore, my brothers whom I love and long for, my joy and crown, stand firm thus in the Lord, my beloved. (Phil. 4:1)

♦ But we were gentle among you, like a nursing mother taking care of her own children. So, being affectionately desirous of you, we were ready to share with you not only the gospel of God but also our own selves, because you had become very dear to us. (1 Thess. 2:7-8)

♦ For I wrote to you out of much affliction and anguish of heart and with many tears, not to cause you pain but to let you know the abundant love that I have for you. (2 Cor. 2:4)

♦ I do not say this to condemn you, for I said before that you are in our hearts, to die together and to live together. (2 Cor. 7:3)

♦ Here for the third time I am ready to come to you. And I will not be a burden, for I seek not what is yours but you. For children are not obligated to save up for their parents, but parents for their children. I will most gladly spend and be spent for your souls. If I love you more, am I to be loved less? (2 Cor. 12:14-15)

♦ My little children, for whom I am again in the anguish of childbirth until Christ is formed in you! (Gal. 4:19)

♦ I am sending him [Onesimus] back to you, sending my very heart. (Philem. 12)

a. Choosing from the entire selection of verses, write down the four statements that you think most powerfully demonstrate Paul's selfless, self-sacrificing love for his converts.

b. What in the above passages of Scripture will help you improve your teaching or leading ministry with people?

Reflections

"Not yours, but you" is the motto of every minister who has learned of Christ.

James Denny

Lesson Three

The Character and Behavior of a Loving Leader

This lesson covers pages 39 to 53 of *Leading with Love*. Read these pages before doing the lesson.

Begin Your Session by Reading the Passages Below

Love is patient and kind; love does not envy or boast; it is not arrogant or rude. It does not insist on its own way; it is not irritable or resentful; it does not rejoice at wrongdoing, but rejoices with the truth. Love bears all things, believes all things, hopes all things, endures all things. (1 Cor. 13:4-7)

We put no obstacle in anyone's way, so that no fault may be found with our ministry, but as servants of God we commend ourselves in every way...by...patience, kindness, the Holy Spirit, genuine love. (2 Cor. 6:3-4, 6)

And we urge you, brothers, admonish the idle, encourage the faint-hearted, help the weak, be patient with them all. (1 Thess. 5:14)

And the Lord's servant must not be quarrelsome but kind to everyone, able to teach, patiently enduring evil, correcting his opponents with gentleness. (2 Tim. 2:24-25)

Chapter 4: Patient and Kind

1. What does the author mean when he says, "in Christian ministry, character is everything" (page 41)?

Reflections

One of the most important chapters in the Bible for life in the local church and for Christian leadership is 1 Corinthians 13. It defines how we should behave in marriage, friendship, church, and society.

Leading with Love, page 41

Review Paul's fifteen descriptions of love:

1. Patient
2. Kind

---

3. Not envious	Delights in the successes and talents of others
4. Not boastful	Promotes others
5. Not arrogant	Is humble and modest
6. Not rude	Displays proper decorum
7. Not selfish	Is self-sacrificing
8. Not easily angered	Calm
9. Not unforgiving	Forgives
10. Not joyful over wrongdoing	11. Rejoices with the truth

---

12. Bears all things
13. Believes all things
14. Hopes all things
15. Endures all things

2. Which two of the fifteen qualities do you, as a leader or teacher, need to be most concerned about in order to improve your character as a Christian leader? Explain your answer.

3. What does the word *patience* mean as used in 1 Corinthians 13:4?

4. What do the following verses teach you about patience?

1 Thessalonians 5:14

2 Corinthians 6:3-4, 6

Galatians 5:22

Ephesians 4:1-2

2 Timothy 4:2

5. List three reasons why patience is a critically important element to leading and teaching people.

Reflections

If we were to ask our Lord, "What is a loving Christian leader like?" he would first answer, "patient and kind." So Paul begins and ends his love catalog with the patient, enduring nature of love (1 Cor. 13:4, 7).

Leading with Love, page 41

---

6. What is meant by the statement that patience is "not passivity?" Provide an example for your answer.

7. In church leadership, we have to deal with many different types of people. What practical steps can you take to help develop patience in your dealings with people, especially difficult ones?

8. a. Define the word *kindness*. Use a dictionary if needed.

b. For a beautiful story of God's kindness displayed through one of his servants, read the account of King David's kindness to Mephibosheth, Jonathan's son, King Saul's grandson (2 Sam. 9). List the ways in which David showed kindness to Mephibosheth. Read 2 Samuel 9.

9. The book states:

Acts of kindness impact people in big ways and capture their attention: a card sent to one who is sick, a concerned phone call, an invitation to dinner, a readiness to help relieve a burden, a caring voice, a gentle touch, a thoughtful gesture, a simple expression of interest in another's concerns, a visit. (*Leading with Love*, page 46)

a. Of the list of acts of kindness in the above paragraph, which two do you find easy to do for others? Explain why.

b. Identify areas in your leadership or teaching ministry in which you should improve your acts of kindness toward others. What exactly would you do to improve?

Chapter 5: Not Envious or Boastful

10. Below is a list of the sins and problems in the church at Corinth. In your thinking, which sins most demonstrate the believers' lack of love for one another? List them and explain your choices.

- party rivalries over teachers,
- love for worldly wisdom,
- lawsuits among believers,
- neglect of church discipline,
- sexual immorality,
- egotistical displays of spiritual gifts and knowledge,
- disorderly conduct in the congregational meetings,
- social snobbery and discrimination against the poor at the Lord's Supper,
- drunkenness at the Lord's Supper,
- conflict over food offered to idols and participation at pagan feasts,
- arrogant individuals criticizing Paul's ministry and teaching,
- denial, by some, of the bodily resurrection and a false view of spirituality, thinking they were presently living in an exalted spiritual state.

Reflections

These eight vices are totally incompatible with love. In brief, they express the self-centered life that tears apart relationships and spoils the unity that should characterize every local church. Paul's list serves as an objective standard to correct our selfish behaviors and to guide us on the "more excellent way."

Leading with Love, page 48

11. Define the word *envy*.

12. To overcome the destructive spirit of envy in his own life, George Muller wrote:

> When in the year 1832, I saw how some preferred my beloved friend's ministry to my own, I determined, in the strength of God, to rejoice in this, instead of envying him. I said, with John the Baptist, "A man can receive nothing, except it be given him from heaven" (John 3:27). This resisting the devil, hindered separation of heart.

What does John 3:27 teach that helped George Muller overcome his envy of his multi-gifted friend Henry Craik? Be sure to consider the full context (John 3:22-36).

13. Whenever you sense the destructive sin of envy arising in your heart toward another, what steps does the author recommend you take to deal with this sin?

14. Why is boasting particularly harmful to a Christian leader?

15. What is the difference between sinful bragging and sharing news about one's life and ministry? (See Acts 14:27; 15:3; Gal. 2:1-14.)

Reflections

Boasting does not build up or serve the church community. Boasting does not honor Christ. Rather, it intimidates and it divides people. It provokes others to envy. Boasting is particularly abhorrent in a leader. It mars a leader's character. We wouldn't want people in the church to follow such an example.

Leading with Love, page 52

---

16. When you are tempted to boast or talk too much about yourself, what specific steps can you take to stop boasting? (See Rom. 12:3-4; 1 Cor. 1:30-31; 3:5-23; Gal. 5:25-26; 6:3-5.)

The Character and Behavior of a Loving Leader

This lesson covers pages 55 to 70 of *Leading with Love*. Read these pages before doing the lesson.

Begin Your Session by Reading the Passages Below

For by the grace given to me I say to everyone among you not to think of himself more highly than he ought to think, but to think with sober judgment, each according to the measure of faith that God has assigned.... Let love be genuine.... Live in harmony with one another. Do not be haughty, but associate with the lowly. Never be conceited. (Rom. 12:3, 9, 16)

Do nothing from rivalry or conceit, but in humility count others more significant than yourselves. Let each of you look not only to his own interests, but also to the interests of others. Have this mind among yourselves, which is yours in Christ Jesus, who, though he was in the form of God, did not count equality with God a thing to be grasped, but made himself nothing, taking the form of a servant, being born in the likeness of men. And being found in human form, he humbled himself by becoming obedient to the point of death, even death on a cross. (Phil. 2:3-8)

Now the works of the flesh are evident: ...enmity, strife, jealousy, fits of anger, rivalries, dissensions, divisions, envy. (Gal. 5:19-21)

But the fruit of the Spirit is love, joy, peace, patience, kindness, goodness, faithfulness, gentleness, self-control. (Gal. 5:22-23)

Chapter 6: Not Arrogant or Rude

1. **a.** Define the word *arrogance* as used by Paul in 1 Cor. 13:4.

b. List several reasons why arrogant self-importance has no place in the life and ministry of a Christian leader or teacher.

Reflections

Those who think too much of themselves don't think enough.

Amy Carmichael

---

2. Diotrephes was a church leader, but not a loving church leader. List Diotrephes' leadership flaws.

I [John] have written something to the church, but Diotrephes, who likes to put himself first, does not acknowledge our authority. So if I come, I will bring up what he is doing, talking wicked nonsense against us. And not content with that, he refuses to welcome the brothers, and also stops those who want to and puts them out of the church. (3 John 9-10)

3. If you have even some small measure of the spirit of Diotrephes in your heart (and many more people have Diotrephes' control problem than we like to admit), what can you do to help yourself? Are there any Scriptures that can help you avoid the urge to control others in unhealthy ways?

Reflections

It was through Pride that the devil became the devil: Pride leads to every other vice: it is the completely anti-God state of mind.

C. S. Lewis

---

4. What do the following Scripture texts teach about how God views pride?

Psalm 31:23

Proverbs 6:16; 8:13; 16:5; Psalm 101:5

Amos 6:8

Mark 7:21-23

2 Corinthians 12:7-9

James 4:6; 1 Peter 5:5

5. Why is humility so vitally important to a Christian teacher? (See also pages 128-129.) List several reasons.

6. What most impacted your thinking about humility as you read the examples of C. S. Lewis's humble-mindedness? Explain.

7. Christian people are to actively humble themselves and behave with humility (Matt. 23:12; Luke 14:11; 18:14; James 4:10; 1 Peter 5:5-6). What kinds of things can you, as a Christian leader, do to display genuine humility in relationship to the people you lead?

Reflections

Humility is the mindset of a servant. It makes a leader more teachable, more receptive to constructive criticism, better able to work with others, better qualified to deal with other people's failures and sins, more willing to submit to others, less prone to fight, and quicker to reconcile differences. Without humility, one cannot be a Christlike leader.

Leading with Love, page 57

----

8. Define the word *rude.*

9. As the coarseness of society worsens around us, what can you do in your home and church to resist this social problem?

Reflections

Loving people are considerate of how their behavior affects others, even in little things. Those who are possessed of God's love are sensitive to proper social relationships, public decency, social convention, politeness, tact, and proper conduct in dress, speech, and action.

Leading with Love, page 60

Chapter 7: Not Selfish or Easily Angered

10. James and John were "card-carrying members of the 'self-seekers' club." What was wrong with James and John wanting to sit on thrones at the right and left hand of Jesus Christ in His glory? See Mark 10:35-45.

11. Barnabas serves as an excellent example of loving leadership. List some of his unselfish acts of love from the following passages.

Acts 4:36-37

Acts 11:19-30

Acts 13:1-5

Reflections

Love is the giving impulse.

Robert Law

---

12. What can you do to act more like Barnabas in your ministry of leading or teaching people? Be specific.

Reflections

Barnabas was not a throne seeker; he was a washer of feet (John 13:14). He was a lifter of people, not a limiter of people (Acts 11:19-24). He was a giver, not a taker. His love was the "giving variety," not the "getting variety."

Leading with Love, page 65

---

13. What does Henry Drummond mean when he says that anger is "the vice of the virtuous" (page 68)?

14. Sinful displays of anger accentuate problems, cloud people's judgment, distort reality, inflame emotions, deepen resentments, hinder peaceful problem solving, and provide the devil a prime opportunity to divide people (Eph. 4:26-27). Uncontrolled anger is a primary reason why so many people are overcome by evil in their relationships with their Christian brothers and sisters (Rom. 12:21).

Using the verses below, describe what the Bible says about sinful displays of anger.

Proverbs 15:18

Proverbs 29:22

Ephesians 4:26-27

Colossians 3:8

Galatians 5:19-20

Titus 1:5, 7

James 1:19-20

15. In sharp contrast to uncontrolled anger, wrath, bitterness, abusive speech, hot tempers, and cutting words, the Scripture encourages calmness, controlled anger, gentle talk, self-control, a cool and gracious spirit, healing words, and wise speech. Only by following scriptural principles of conduct can we hope to enjoy healthy group relationships and provide Christlike leadership for God's flock.

Take some time to read and consider the following passages. List the two key passages that you think will be most beneficial in helping you improve your ability to handle difficult people and situations without resorting to destructive anger. Briefly explain your choices.

- The tongue of the wise brings healing. (Prov. 12:18)
- Whoever is slow to anger has great understanding. (Prov. 14:29)
- A soft answer turns away wrath, but a harsh word stirs up anger. (Prov. 15:1)
- A gentle tongue [speaking words that heal] is a tree of life. (Prov. 15:4)
- He who is slow to anger quiets contention. (Prov. 15:18)
- Whoever restrains his words has knowledge, and he who has a cool spirit is a man of understanding. (Prov. 17:27)
- It is an honor for a man to keep aloof from strife, but every fool will be quarreling. (Prov. 20:3)
- A soft tongue will break a bone. (Prov. 25:15)
- The wise turn away wrath. (Prov. 29:8)
- Let your speech always be gracious, seasoned with salt, so that you may know how you ought to answer each person. (Col. 4:6)
- Who is wise and understanding among you? By his good conduct let him show his works in the meekness of wisdom. (James 3:13)

Lesson Five

The Character and Behavior of a Loving Leader

This lesson covers pages 71 to 88 of *Leading with Love*. Read these pages before doing the lesson.

Begin Your Session by Reading the Passages Below

It does not rejoice at wrongdoing, but rejoices with the truth. Love bears all things, believes all things, hopes all things, endures all things. Love never ends. As for prophecies, they will pass away; as for tongues, they will cease; as for knowledge, it will pass away.... So now faith, hope, and love abide, these three; but the greatest of these is love. (1 Cor. 13:6-8, 13)

Pursue love, and earnestly desire the spiritual gifts. (1 Cor. 14:1)

Bearing with one another and, if one has a complaint against another, forgiving each other; as the Lord has forgiven you, so you also must forgive. And above all these put on love, which binds everything together in perfect harmony. (Col. 3:13-14)

I do not say this to condemn you, for I said before that you are in our hearts, to die together and to live together. I am acting with great boldness toward you; I have great pride in you; I am filled with comfort. In all our affliction, I am overflowing with joy.... I rejoice, because I have perfect confidence in you. (2 Cor. 7:3-4, 16)

Therefore love truth. (Zech. 8:19)

43

Chapter 8: Not Resentful or Joyful over Evil

1. Carefully define the word *resentful*. Be sure you understand the meaning of this significant term.

2. Why is this quality of love ("not resentful") particularly important to a Christian leader?

3. People involved in leadership often experience deep emotional hurts inflicted by those they lead. What steps can be taken to properly deal with the emotional hurts and injustices inflicted by other people? (See pages 73-74.) Write out your answers in list form and don't rush over this question. It is vital to your ministry with people that you know how to correctly handle emotional wounds.

Reflections

We all have been hurt by evil inflicted on us by others. We all have had to struggle with forgiveness. We all have had to let go of bad memories and give up any desire for revenge in order to be reconciled with those who have injured us. There is no way we could live happily together in marriage or with other believers in the local church without this quality of love. If we refuse to let go of emotional hurts, if we enjoy nursing old wounds, if we feel compelled to get even with our enemies, we will be devoured by bitterness, anger, and unforgiveness. We will be miserable examples and ineffective leaders for Christ.

Leading with Love, pages 72-3

4. In Chapter 8 there are eight stories, starting with R. C. Chapman and ending with John Perkins, about love and forgiveness. Which one of these stories most convicted you about the necessity of forgiving those who have hurt you? Explain your choice.

5. What do the following verses teach about Christian forgiveness?

Matthew 6:14-15

Matthew 18:21-22

Luke 17:3-4

Luke 23:34

Acts 7:60

2 Corinthians 2:6-8, 11

Ephesians 4:32

Colossians 3:13

Reflections

To forgive without upbraiding, even by manner or look, is a high exercise of grace—it is imitation of Christ.

Robert Chapman

---

6. **a.** Explain why love cannot rejoice in unrighteousness of any kind.

b. In what subtle ways do you find yourself rejoicing over others' misfortune or at the news of religious scandal? Give examples from your own inner thought life of rejoicing over others' misfortune or public scandal.

7. **a.** What does the word *truth* mean in the context of verse 6?

b. Give an example from your experience of rejoicing "with the truth."

_____

Reflections

What a man rejoices in is a fair test of his character. To be glad when evil prevails, or to rejoice in the misfortunes of others is indicative of great moral degradation.

W. G. Scroggie

_____

Chapter 9: Bears, Believes, Hopes, and Endures All Things

8. Although the details of verse 7 can be difficult to understand, what is the main point of this verse?

9. In what ways does Moses' leadership of the rebellious nation of Israel through the wilderness for forty years illustrate the following statements concerning love? (See pages 84-85 and be sure you understand each of the four statements before you answer the question.)

"bears all things"

"believes all things"

"hopes all things"

"endures all things"

Reflections

Most significant ministry with people is usually long-term, but long-term ministry succeeds only with supernatural power from above to endure all of life's hardships and heartaches. Some missionaries serve for decades in dangerous areas where the problems and setbacks never end. How do they last? The answer: love for God and love for people. Love generates the faith, hope, and endurance to persevere through a lifetime of problems.

Leading with Love, page 85

---

10. What is the main point Paul makes about love and spiritual gifts in 1 Corinthians 13:8-12? How should your answer affect the life of your local church?

11. The author pleads with his readers not to use this book to tell other people that they have no love. Why do you think the author is so emphatic about this point?

12. When it is necessary for teachers and leaders to address the problem of lovelessness (and at times it is necessary), what is the proper way to do so?

13. a. It has often been said that you can substitute the name *Jesus* for *love* throughout the following passage. So try it. Place the name Jesus or Jesus Christ in the spaces below. Read it this way once during your group session.

_____ is patient and _____ [is] kind; _____ does not envy or boast; _____ is not arrogant; _____ [is not] rude. _____does not insist on [his or her] own way; _____ is not irritable; _____ [is not] resentful; _____ does not rejoice at wrongdoing, but rejoices with the truth. _____ bears all things, _____ believes all things, _____ hopes all things, _____ endures all things. (1 Cor. 13:4-7)

b. God's will is for his people to be like his Son Jesus Christ and to love as he loved, so we can apply this passage personally by placing our own name for love in each blank. Hopefully your friends wouldn't laugh when they hear you read this passage aloud with your name inserted. Of course, if they do laugh, read it aloud with their name inserted in the blanks. They won't laugh anymore!

By doing this exercise, you will now learn how to act and think in the spirit of love. Try this a few times in your group session until you get the idea of what God is expecting from you and me.

_____ is patient and _____ [is] kind; _____ does not envy or boast; _____ is not arrogant; _____ [is not] rude. _____does not insist on [his or her] own way; _____ is not irritable; _____ [is not] resentful; _____ does not rejoice at wrongdoing, but rejoices with the truth. _____ bears all things, _____ believes all things, _____ hopes all things, _____ endures all things. (1 Cor. 13:4-7)

c. Now substitute the name of your leadership or ministry position for the word love. For example, say "An elder is patient..." or, " A teacher is patient...".

_____ is patient and _____ [is] kind; _____ does not envy or boast; _____ is not arrogant; _____ [is not] rude. _____ does not insist on [his or her] own way; _____ is not irritable; _____ [is not] resentful; _____ does not rejoice at wrongdoing, but rejoices with the truth. _____ bears all things, _____ believes all things, _____ hopes all things, _____ endures all things. (1 Cor. 13:4-7)

d. Finally, marriage is the first place to implement the Christian characteristics of love as described in 1 Corinthians 13:4-7, so apply this passage to your marriage relationship. Substitute the name "a Christian husband" or "a Christian wife" for the word love. Marriage is the fundamental testing and proving ground of love. A Christian leader can't love people in the church, but hate the spouse at home. That is hypocrisy, and the Scripture says, "Let love be without hypocrisy" (Rom. 12:9; NASB).

_____ is patient and _____ [is] kind; _____ does not envy or boast; _____ is not arrogant; _____ [is not] rude. _____ does not insist on [his or her] own way; _____ is not irritable; _____ [is not] resentful; _____ does not rejoice at wrongdoing, but rejoices with the truth. _____ bears all things, _____ believes all things, _____ hopes all things, _____ endures all things. (1 Cor. 13:4-7)

These love qualities will make you more skilled in serving people, so let them shape your character. As they do, you will be more like the loving Lord Jesus Christ.

14. Based on what you have learned from 1 Corinthians 13:1-7, briefly describe the character and behavior of a loving leader.

Reflections

When Christians love one another as Jesus did, the local church family prefigures the glories of our future loving, heavenly existence. Sadly, the church at Corinth was not experiencing heavenly love. It was characterized by rivalries, lawsuits, immorality, abuse of Christian liberty, disorderly conduct, pride, and selfish independence—altogether an unacceptably poor representation of the heavenly realities of love and the fruit of the Spirit.

Leading with Love, page 86

The Works
of a Loving Leader

This lesson covers pages 91 to 105 of *Leading with Love*. Read these
pages before doing the lesson.

Begin Your Session by Reading the Passages Below

My love be with you all in Christ Jesus. (1 Cor. 16:24)

I yearn for you all with the affection of Christ Jesus. (Phil. 1:8)

*I wrote to you...to let you know the abundant love that I have for
you.* (2 Cor. 2:4)

*Let love be genuine.... Love one another with brotherly affection....
Seek to show hospitality.* (Rom. 12:9, 10, 13)

*Let brotherly love continue. Do not neglect to show hospitality to
strangers, for thereby some have entertained angels unawares.*
(Heb. 13:1-2)

*Above all, keep loving one another earnestly.... Show hospitality to
one another ...without grumbling.* (1 Peter 4:8-9)

Chapter 10: Expressing Love and Affection

1. What actions and character traits does Paul acknowledge and praise in
Romans 16? From the verses below, list as many as you can. Don't sim-
ply repeat the words of the texts; use your own words to describe what
Paul acknowledges and praises.

- ◆ Phoebe, a servant of the church (Rom. 16:1)
- ◆ Prisca and Aquila...who risked their necks for my life (Rom. 16:3-4)
- ◆ Mary, who has worked hard for you (Rom. 16:6)
- ◆ Andronicus and Junia....They are well known to the apostles
  (Rom. 16:7)
- ◆ Ampliatus, my beloved in the Lord (Rom. 16:8)
- ◆ Apelles, who is approved in Christ (Rom. 16:10)
- ◆ Those workers in the Lord Tryphaena and Tryphosa (Rom. 16:12)
- ◆ The beloved Persis, who has worked hard in the Lord (Rom. 16:12)
- ◆ Rufus, chosen in the Lord (Rom. 16:13)
- ◆ Gaius, who is host to me and to the whole church (Rom. 16:23)

2. **a.** How would you answer someone who says there is no need to
acknowledge or thank people for their service because they are doing
their work for God and God is the one who is responsible to reward
and acknowledge his people for faithful service (Matt. 25:21)?

b. How would you respond to someone who says we will cause people to be tempted with pride if we publicly praise their work or character?

3. List specific ways you can acknowledge and thank people in your church or group for their faithful service to others or their quality of Christian character.

4. The following passages display Paul's loving heart and affectionate leadership style. Which two passages most touched your heart regarding Paul's intense love for his converts? Explain your choices.

- ◆ I rejoice over you. (Rom. 16:19)
- ◆ I hold you in my heart. (Phil. 1:7)
- ◆ I yearn for you all with the affection of Christ Jesus. (Phil. 1:8)
- ◆ My brothers, whom I love and long for, my joy and crown. (Phil. 4:1)
- ◆ Being affectionately desirous of you, we were ready to share with you not only the gospel of God but also our own selves, because you had become very dear to us. (1 Thess. 2:8)
- ◆ My little children, for whom I am again in the anguish of childbirth until Christ is formed in you. (Gal. 4:19)
- ◆ My love be with you all in Christ Jesus. (1 Cor. 16:24)
- ◆ I wrote to you out of much affliction and anguish of heart and with many tears...to let you know the abundant love that I have for you. (2 Cor. 2:4)

- ◆ We have spoken freely to you, Corinthians; our heart is wide open. (2 Cor. 6:11)
- ◆ You are in our hearts, to die together and to live together. (2 Cor. 7:3)
- ◆ Because I do not love you? God knows I do! (2 Cor. 11:11)
- ◆ I seek not what is yours but you. (2 Cor. 12:14)
- ◆ I will most gladly spend and be spent for your souls. If I love you more, am I to be loved less? (2 Cor. 12:15)
- ◆ And may the Lord make you increase...in love for one another...as we do for you. (1 Thess. 3:12)
- ◆ I am sending him back to you, sending my very heart [the slave Onesimus]. (Philem. 12)

5. What endearing terms can you use, without being phony or uncomfortable, to express your love for those you teach and lead?

6. What does the author mean when he says the local church "is to be a life-transforming community?"

7. List ways that you and your fellow leaders can help believers grow in love. Answer this question with the intent of taking positive action in accordance with the answers you give. This is not meant to be an exchange of creative theories.

The local church is "the household of God" (1 Tim. 3:15) and should be filled with loving words and demonstrations of familial affection. Sadly, the atmosphere in some churches is more like a funeral home than a loving family home. There is little affection and warmth. Legitimate emotional feelings are suffocated. People hardly know one another. They keep their distance, and the only display of affection is a speedy handshake before exiting the church doors. Such behavior is not authentic, Christian brotherhood and sisterhood.

Leading with Love, page 96

Chapter 11: Practicing Hospitality

8. Briefly explain each of the following statements below. Point out key words and ideas in each one. If you have commentaries on these passages, use them. Or, if you have *The Hospitality Commands* by Alexander Strauch, it will also help you understand these passages.[1] *The Hospitality Commands* is a short, 53-page booklet that can be given to each of the leaders in your church or group to help them understand loving, Christian hospitality.

Romans 12:13: "Seek to show hospitality."

1 Peter 4:9: "Show hospitality to one another without grumbling."

Hebrews 13:2: "Do not neglect to show hospitality to strangers, for thereby some have entertained angels unawares."

3 John 5-6: "Beloved, it is a faithful thing you [Gaius] do in all your efforts for these brothers [missionaries and preachers], strangers as they are, who testified to your love [hospitality] before the church." Why is John, the apostle, so delighted with Gaius?

1 Timothy 3:2: "Therefore an overseer [elder] must be above reproach, the husband of one wife, sober-minded, self-controlled, respectable, hospitable." (also Titus 1:8)

9. List three reasons why hospitality is a biblical requirement for a church elder (or overseer).

Reflections

You don't have to be a preacher or have years of training to use your home to love and serve people. If you simply open the doors of your home, the people will come.

Leading with Love, page 103

---

10. From your own experience, explain why teaching people or being taught in a home environment is a powerfully effective way to communicate the Word of God.

11. Give several examples of how hospitality can be used for evangelism.

12. List at least three rich benefits you and your family will receive if you practice hospitality.

13. If you have had a memorable or funny experience while practicing hospitality or being treated to hospitality, share your story with the group.

14. What most hinders you from actively practicing hospitality?

From the following list of hindrances to hospitality, pick two that apply to you. Write out some simple steps you can take to overcome these problems and become more hospitable.

_____ Time pressures (too many other things to do)
_____ Finances
_____ Inadequate living conditions
_____ Selfishness
_____ Fear of failure
_____ Inexperience
_____ Lack of discipline and organization (or failure to plan ahead)
_____ Pride
_____ Others

15. On pages 103-105, there is a list of suggestions to help you obey the command of Scripture to practice hospitality. Which of these ideas is most helpful to you? Why?

16. Fill in the blanks of this quotation, "Christian hospitality is not a matter of _____ ; it is not a matter of _____ ; it is not a matter of _____ , _____ , _____ , or _____ . Christian hospitality is a matter of _____ to God."

Helga Henry

Suggested Assignment

An excellent article to read and make available to your church leaders is, "A Friendly Church is Hard to Find," by Gene and Nancy Preston in the *Christian Century* (January 30, 1991). You can download it at www.lewisandroth.org.

---

[1] Alexander Strauch, *The Hospitality Commands: Building Loving Christian Community and Building Bridges to Friends and Neighbors* (Littleton, CO., Lewis and Roth, 1993).

Lesson Seven

The Works
of a Loving Leader

This lesson covers pages 107 to 124 of *Leading with Love.* **Read these pages before doing the lesson.**

Begin Your Session by Reading the Passages Below

*Let love be genuine.... Love one another with brotherly affection....
Contribute to the needs of the saints. (Rom. 12:9-10, 13)*

*So give proof before the churches of your love [their love offering for the
poor in Jerusalem] and of our boasting about you to these men. (2 Cor. 8:24)*

*Praying at all times in the Spirit, with all prayer and supplication. To that
end keep alert with all perseverance, making supplication for all the saints,
and also for me, that words may be given to me in opening my mouth
boldly to proclaim the mystery of the gospel, for which I am an ambassador
in chains, that I may declare it boldly, as I ought to speak. (Eph. 6:18-20)*

*Therefore, confess yours sins to one another and pray for one another, that
you may be healed. The prayer of a righteous person has great power as it
is working. (James 5:16)*

*For he who does not love his brother whom he has seen cannot love
God whom he has not seen. And this commandment we have from
him: whoever loves God must also love his brother. (1 John 4:20-21)*

63

Chapter 12: Caring for Peoples' Needs

Read below the story of the Good Samaritan:

> A man was going down from Jerusalem to Jericho, and he fell among robbers, who stripped him and beat him and departed, leaving him half dead. Now by chance a priest was going down that road, and when he saw him he passed by on the other side. So likewise a Levite, when he came to the place and saw him, passed by on the other side. But a Samaritan, as he journeyed, came to where he was, and when he saw him, he had compassion. He went to him and bound up his wounds, pouring on oil and wine. Then he set him on his own animal and brought him to an inn and took care of him. And the next day he took out two denarii and gave them to the innkeeper, saying, "Take care of him and whatever more you spend, I will repay you when I come back." (Luke 10:30-35)

1. **a.** What did it cost the Good Samaritan personally to help an unknown, dying man on the road to Jericho? List as many things as you can.

   b. Considering the cultural and religious context, what excuses did the priest and Levite use for refusing to help the dying man on the road to Jericho?

   c. What sins did the priest and Levite commit by refusing to help a fellow human being in desperate need?

2. What vital truths does Jesus Christ teach his followers by means of the story of the Good Samaritan? To answer this question, read the full context of the story (Luke 10:25-37).

3. What do you honestly think you would have done if you had found the dying man on the road to Jericho? Would you have done as much as the Good Samaritan did? Or would you have done much less?

4. a. Why is it important that a Christian leader be genuinely concerned about sick or dying people in the congregation? List as many reasons as you can.

b. What do you personally do for sick or dying people in your church?

5. What does the author mean by "We must all be aware of and look out for the growing senior population" (page 111)? What does this statement have to do with your church and its future?

6. What practical steps can you take (personally and corporately) to help busy, over-burdened people become more aware of and mobilized to care for the church's sick, shut-ins, and poor? Remember Acts 6:1-6.

Reflections

A leader will not have much of a ministry if people do not know that he or she truly cares about them. So a leader needs to demonstrate a tender heart toward suffering members, a genuine concern for the sick, a generous disposition to the poor, and a spirit of mercy to help relieve the misery that characterizes the lives of so many people today.

Leading with Love, page 109

---

7. John best describes the standard of love among believers envisioned by the New Testament:

> By this we know love, that he laid down his life for us, and we ought to lay down our lives for the brothers. But if anyone has the world's goods and sees his brother in need, yet closes his heart [refuses to show compassion] against him, how does God's love abide in him? Little children, let us not love in word or talk but in deed and in truth. (1 John 3:16-18)

a. How would you describe this standard of love?

b. What does John mean by the words, "yet closes his heart against him"?

c. Why is closing one's heart to the needs of others such a serious matter to the beloved disciple John?

d. According to 1 John 3:16-18, how is Christlike love and compassion to be displayed?

8. What does the author mean by the statement, "Loving leaders find themselves making lots of phone calls" (page110)? How would the truth of this statement help you be a more effective, loving leader?

9. Job is a wonderful example of a compassionate, loving leader. Read his own testimony to his big-hearted compassion for poor and needy people:

"Did not I weep for him whose day was hard?
Was not my soul grieved for the needy?" (Job 30:25)

"Because I delivered the poor who cried for help,
and the fatherless who had none to help him.
The blessing of him who was about to perish came upon me,
and I caused the widow's heart to sing for joy.
I put on righteousness, and it clothed me;
my justice was like a robe and a turban.
I was eyes to the blind and feet to the lame.
I was a father to the needy,
and I searched out the cause of him who I did not know."
                                                    (Job 29:12-16)

"If I have witheld anything that the poor desired,
or have caused the eyes of the widow to fail,
or have eaten my morsel alone,
and the fatherless has not eaten of it...
if I have seen anyone perish for lack of clothing,
or the needy without covering....
then let my shoulder blade fall from my shoulder,
and let my arm be broken from its socket." (Job 31:16-17, 19, 22)

a. List the kinds of people Job cared for in their "affliction."

b. From the passage above, describe in your own words Job's disposition toward suffering people.

c. List all the things that Job did for needy people.

d. What practical steps can you take to begin to develop a compassionate heart like Job's (and the Lord Jesus Christ)?

Reflections

As leaders and teachers, we can make a difference. We can cast a vision and set an example of compassionate care. We can raise awareness and set up organizational structures providing opportunities for people to share with others in need. We can also warn of how materialism, prosperity, and greed harden the heart and blind our eyes to the terrible suffering of our fellow believers as well as that of other human beings.

Leading with Love, pages 113-114

Chapter 13: Laboring in Prayer

10. D. Martyn Lloyd Jones reminds us that prayer can be one of the most difficult things we do in the Christian life:

> When a man is speaking to God he is at his very acme. It is the highest activity of the human soul, and therefore it is at the same time the ultimate test of a man's true spiritual condition. There is nothing that tells the truth about us as Christian people so much as our prayer life. Everything we do in the Christian life is easier than prayer.

a. Why do you think, "Everything we do in the Christian life is easier than prayer"? What makes consistent prayer so difficult for us?

b. Explain how love for God and neighbor affects praying for others.

11. What do the following passages of Scripture teach you about prayer and your prayers as a leader?

1 Samuel 12:23

Mark 1:35

Luke 11:1

Luke 18:1

Luke 22:31-32

Acts 6:4

Romans 10:1

Romans 15:30-31

2 Corinthians 1:10-11

Ephesians 1:16

Ephesians 6:18-20

Philippians 4:6-7

1 Thessalonians 5:17-18

1 Thessalonians 5:25

1 Timothy 2:1-2

Hebrews 4:16

James 5:16-17

12. What are some practical ways you can draw out needed prayer requests from those you lead and teach in order to stimulate and enhance your prayers for them?

Reflections

To pray intelligently, we need information; we need current prayer requests.

Leading with Love, page 121

---

13. a. If you do not have an intercessory prayer list to help you pray systematically and consistently for those you lead and teach, think of how you would organize and implement such a prayer list. Get started, even if you begin with just a few names.

b. List a few biblical statements from the prayers found on pages 122-123 that you can use as you pray for the people you presently lead.

Reflections

Out of love for those you lead, commit yourself to improving your intercessory prayer. Ask yourself, *If those I lead were dependent on my prayers, how would they do?* Or, *If our missionaries were dependent on my prayers, how would they do?*

Leading with Love, pages 123-124

---

14. Take some time now, with your study group, to share practical ideas for improving your intercessory prayer ministry for others. Help each other with fresh ideas and start anew to pray consistently, persistently, and intelligently for others.

Reflections

The best teachers and preachers labor to improve their teaching skills, and they should. Competent leaders and administrators seek to continually improve their leadership abilities, and they should. So, too, believer priests should labor to improve their intercessory prayer ministry.

Leading with Love, page 121

Lesson Eight

The Works
of a Loving Leader

This lesson covers pages 125 to 142 from *Leading with Love*. Stop your reading at the bottom of page 142 before "How to Warn and Rebuke with Love." The rest of the chapter will be covered in the next lesson. Read pages 125-142 before doing the lesson.

Begin Your Session by Reading the Passages Below

I will give you shepherds after my own heart, who will feed you with knowledge and understanding. (Jer. 3:15)

When he went ashore he saw a great crowd, and he had compassion on them, because they were like sheep without a shepherd. And he began to teach them many things. (Mark 6:34)

And the Lord's servant must not be quarrelsome but kind to everyone, able to teach, patiently enduring evil, correcting his opponents with gentleness. (2 Tim. 2:24-25)

Have I then become your enemy by telling you the truth? (Gal. 4:16)

Therefore be alert, remembering that for three years I did not cease night or day to admonish everyone with tears. (Acts 20:31)

To write the same things to you is no trouble to me and is safe for you.

Look out for the dogs, look out for the evildoers, look out for those who mutilate the flesh. (Phil. 3:1-2)

Chapter 14: Feeding Hungry Souls

1. Explain the meaning of Deuteronomy 8:3. (Remember to consult the full context and see also Matthew 4:4; John 6:49-51.) Why is this an important verse of Scripture for leaders and teachers to know?

2. Why does love compel us to teach the Word of God to others? List as many reasons as you can.

3. Fill in the following blanks. On page 126 the author states, "Love for people _____ us to preach and teach God's Word." Furthermore, he writes, "Love cannot bear to see loved ones in _____ _____, starving for the _____ _____, and it will not leave them in ignorance."

_____

Reflections

When we see pictures of emaciated, starving children our hearts grieve and we want to help. So, too, our hearts should grieve when we see God's people emaciated and starving spiritually because of a famine of the Word of God. We should want to take immediate action because love always seeks to provide loved ones' needs and the greatest need people have is for the Word of God. The Lord himself

says: "Man does not live by bread alone, but man lives by every word that comes from the mouth of the Lord" (Deut. 8:3).

Leading with Love, pages 125-126

---

4. Explain why a loving, Christian disposition makes a person a better teacher or preacher. Can you give an example of an effective, loving teacher you have encountered?

Reflections

Leadership in the apostolic church was largely based on proper teaching.

William Mounce

---

5. What do you learn about becoming a more loving teacher from each of the following verses of Scripture below? Make a list of specific characteristics of a loving preacher or teacher of the gospel message.

Mark 6:34

Matthew 11:29

2 Corinthians 4:5

2 Corinthians 10:1

1 Thessalonians 2:4

1 Thessalonians 2:5

1 Thessalonians 2:6

1 Thessalonians 2:7

1 Thessalonians 2:8

1 Thessalonians 2:9

1 Thessalonians 2:10

1 Thessalonians 2:11-12

2 Timothy 2:24

2 Timothy 2:25

1 Peter 3:15-16

6. You have now read and studied some important character qualities of a loving teacher. Which qualities do you personally need to incorporate into your own teaching ministry (whether it is informal instruction to a few people or formal teaching and preaching to a large group of people)?

How would you actually make such changes? Share your ideas for change with your study group.

Reflections

Good teachers love their students and give themselves unselfishly to their education. They care about their students. They respect and value them. They know and understand them. Loving teachers are dedicated to their students' education. Like Paul, they can say, "we were ready to share with you not only the gospel of God but also our own selves, because you had become very dear to us" (1 Thess. 2:8).

Leading with Love, page 128

---

7. Reread the significant quotation by Paul Stanley and Robert Clinton:

We have observed that most people cease learning by the age of forty. By that we mean they no longer actively pursue knowledge, understanding, and experience that will enhance their capacity to grow and contribute to others. Most simply rest on what they already know. But those who finish well [life and ministry] maintain a *positive learning attitude* all their lives.

Many people, particularly leaders, plateau. They become satisfied with where they are and with what they know. This often occurs after they attain enough to be comfortable or can maintain a relatively secure and predictable future. But this contradicts the biblical principle of stewardship.

What do the following verses teach you about passionately striving to continually grow in every area of your Christian life and ministry?

Proverbs 1:5

2 Corinthians 3:18

2 Corinthians 4:16

Philippians 3:12-14

1 Timothy 4:7b-8

1 Timothy 4:15

1 Peter 2:2

8. One of the simplest definitions of leadership is: Leadership is influence. If you are not influencing people's thinking, values, ideas, and lifestyle for Jesus Christ, you are not really leading them. However, you cannot influence people for Christ if you are not growing in the knowledge of Christ yourself.

a. Why do you think so many Christians lose their passion for growth in the knowledge of God and Scripture and just rest on what they already know?

Reflections

There is no doubt that the best teachers in any field of knowledge are those who remain students all their lives.

John Stott

b. What do you do presently to continue to learn, grow, change, and move forward in your Christian life and ministry? Be specific and share your thoughts with others in your group.

Reflections

When we lose our zeal for knowledge, we lose our zest for teaching. When we stop growing, we stop influencing others. When we're not excited about Scripture, we don't excite others. If we expect to challenge the hearts and minds of men and women of the next generation, our hearts and minds must be challenged also. We cannot influence people for God if we are not learning, changing, and growing. Teachers who love God and love to study his Word reproduce this love in others.

Leading with Love, page 133

9. A number of suggestions were made to improve your teaching skills. Which one would most help you personally? Explain why.

Reflections

If you are part of a leadership team responsible for leading and teaching people, lay out a clear biblical philosophy of teaching and preaching the Scriptures. Also, regularly evaluate your teaching ministry and plan for the future. Be sure the content of your teaching is biblical, challenging, applicable, and relevant to the people. Don't let it become haphazard or ineffective. Be able to say as Paul did, "I did not shrink from declaring to you the whole purpose of God" (Acts 20:27).

Leading with Love, page 134

Chapter 15: Protecting and Reproving Loved Ones

10. a. Circle all the statements below that *clearly help explain* why Jesus Christ so vehemently denounced the Pharisees and scribes as wolves among the sheep. Explain one of your choices.

- But woe to you, scribes and Pharisees, hypocrites! For you shut the kingdom of heaven in people's faces. (Matt. 23:13)
- Woe to you, blind guides…. (Matt. 23:16)
- So you also outwardly appear righteous to others, but within you are full of hypocrisy and lawlessness. (Matt. 23:28)
- You serpents, you brood of vipers, how are you to escape being sentenced to hell? (Matt. 23:33)
- You have a fine way of rejecting the commandment of God in order to establish your tradition…thus making void the word of God by your tradition. (Mark 7:9, 13)
- Beware of the scribes…who devour widows' houses and for a pretense make long prayers. (Luke 20:46, 47)

b. How would you explain to someone the stern, thunderous denunciations of Jesus Christ (the most loving man to have ever graced this earth) against the religious leaders of his day? Or, how would you defend Jesus Christ from the criticism that he was hateful, intolerant, and bigoted toward the Pharisees and scribes?

11. Using the verses below, describe in detail the personal character, deeds, and sad results of false teachers of the gospel.

Micah 3:11

Jeremiah 14:14

Jeremiah 23:32

Zechariah 10:2

Malachi 2:7-9

Matthew 7:15-20

Matthew 23:28

Mark 7:9, 13

2 Corinthians 11:13-15

Philippians 3:2

Titus 1:10-11

2 Peter 2:1-3

---

12. What did Paul mean when he said to the Ephesian elders, "I testify to you this day that I am innocent of the blood of all of you, for I did not shrink from declaring to you the whole counsel of God" (Acts 20:26-27)? Be sure to read the whole context, Acts 20:17-38.

13. As leaders and teachers of God's people, it is our duty to lovingly correct, warn, or rebuke those we lead. But confronting people's sins and problems is a task most leaders avoid because of the emotional cost. However, it is part of the leadership task, and must be done. What practical steps can you take to improve your personal courage and skills in loving confrontation?

The Works
of a Loving Leader

This lesson covers pages 142 to 164 of *Leading with Love*. Beginning your reading at the bottom of page 142 with "How to Warn and Rebuke with Love." Then proceed on to all of Chapter 16. Read pages 142-164 before doing the lesson.

Begin Your Session by Reading the Passages Below

For the Lord disciplines the one he loves, and chastises every son whom he receives. (Heb. 12:6)

For they [our fathers] disciplined us for a short time as it seemed best to them, but he disciplines us for our good, that we may share in his holiness. For the moment all discipline seems painful rather than pleasant, but later it yields the peaceful fruit of righteousness to those who have been trained by it. (Heb. 12:10-11)

Those whom I love, I reprove and discipline, so be zealous and repent. (Rev. 3:19)

For such a one, this punishment by the majority is enough, so you should rather turn to forgive and comfort him, or he may be overwhelmed by excessive sorrow. So I beg you to reaffirm your love for him. For this is why I wrote, that I might test you and know whether you are obedient in everything. (2 Cor. 2:6-9)

Brothers, if anyone is caught in any transgression, you who are spiritual should restore him in a spirit of gentleness. Keep watch on yourself, lest you too be tempted. (Gal. 6:1)

Chapter 16: Disciplining and Restoring the Wayward

1. How would you explain the seeming contradiction between Paul's stern statements in 1 Corinthians 5 regarding church discipline and his later statements about love in 1 Corinthians 13:4, 7, and 16:14?

- ◆ Let him who has done this be removed from among you. (1 Cor. 5:2)
- ◆ Deliver this man to Satan for the destruction of the flesh, so that his spirit may be saved in the day of the Lord. (1 Cor. 5:5)
- ◆ Cleanse out the old leaven. (1 Cor. 5:7)
- ◆ Not even to eat with such a one. (1 Cor. 5:11)
- ◆ Purge the evil person from among you. (1 Cor. 5:13)

- ◆ Love is patient and kind.... Love bears all things, believes all things, hopes all things, endures all things. (1 Cor. 13:4, 7)
- ◆ Let all that you do be done in love. (1 Cor. 16:14)

Reflections

Love is not just happy smiles or pleasant words. A critical test of genuine love is whether we are willing to confront and discipline those we care for. Nothing is more difficult than disciplining a brother or sister in Christ who is trapped in sin. It is always agonizing work—messy,

complicated, often unsuccessful, emotionally exhausting, and potentially divisive. This is why most church leaders avoid discipline at all costs. But that is not love. It is lack of courage and disobedience to the Lord Jesus Christ, who himself laid down instructions for the discipline of an unrepentant believer.

Leading with Love, page 152

———————

2. Paul had to rebuke the church at Corinth for not taking disciplinary action against one of its impenitent members. This same inaction and complacency regarding dealing with sin exists today. Why do you think most church leaders avoid the practice of corrective church discipline? List as many reason as you can.

3. Certain character qualities are necessary for a leader to be able to initiate and follow through with corrective church discipline. Name some of these qualities.

4. Carefully read 2 Corinthians 2:5-11 below. This is the account of Paul's instruction to the church at Corinth on how to restore the rebellious man who had humiliated Paul and been disciplined by the church.

Now if anyone [the offending brother] has caused pain, he has caused it not to me, but in some measure—not to put it too severely—to all of you. For such a one, this punishment [the discipline] by the majority is enough, so you should rather turn to forgive and comfort him, or he may be overwhelmed by excessive sorrow. So I beg you to reaffirm your love for him. For this is why I wrote, that I might test you and know whether you are obedient in everything. Anyone whom you forgive, I also forgive. What I have forgiven, if I have forgiven anything, has been for your sake in the presence of Christ, so that we would not be outwitted by Satan; for we are not ignorant of his designs.

a. What attitudes does Paul personally display in this passage toward the offender and the church body?

b. What are the key steps and attitudes for restoring one who has been publicly disciplined by the church? (Be sure to read endnote 8.)

c. Explain the meaning of 2 Corinthians 2:11. This verse is imperative to understand when facing the issues of church discipline and restoration.

Reflections

Making proper moral and spiritual judgments about doctrine and conduct is required by Scripture. The gospel would be lost to the world and the church would be assimilated into secular society if we did not make discriminating judgments between truth and error, Christ and Satan. Thus the Scripture commands, "do not believe every spirit, but test the spirits to see whether they are from God, for many false prophets have gone out into the world" (1 John 4:1).

Leading with Love, page 159

5. "Matthew 7:1-5 has become a modern day mantra. People who have never read one word of the Gospels know this verse. It proves to them that Jesus was a teacher of tolerance; he was non-judgmental and non-dogmatic; he would condemn no one; he would never judge anyone" (quoted from pages 157-158).

Since this passage of Scripture is so horribly misused by both non-Christians and Christians to condemn church discipline or any negative moral judgment against another, it is vital that you be able to explain the passage correctly. Feel free to use commentaries to help you understand this passage.

a. What were the Pharisees and scribes doing wrong that prompted Jesus to say, "Judge not, that you be not judged"?

b. What does the following statement, "For with the judgment you pronounce you will be judged, and with the measure you use it will be measured to you," mean?

c. Explain the following verse and provide an example to illustrate your explanation: "Why do you see the speck that is in your brother's eye, but do not notice the log that is in your own eye?"

d. Explain the following verse and provide an example to illustrate your explanation. "Or how can you say to your brother. Let me take the speck out of your eye, when there is the log in your own eye?"

e. Give a more detailed explanation of the meaning of the following verse: "You hypocrite, first take the log out of your own eye, and then you will see clearly to take the speck out of your brother's eye."

6. How does the new "tolerance" movement redefine the word *tolerance?* Give an example. How should the word *tolerance* be defined?

7. How would you explain to a person who prided himself or herself on being open-minded and tolerant, that your church disfellowshipped one of its members because of unrepentant sinful behavior?

Reflections

The word tolerance is being used as a club to intimidate and marginalize people who don't fall to their knees before the god of moral and religious relativism. The word itself is actually used to foster intolerance of all dissenters of secular relativism and its religious counterparts.

Leading with Love, page 162

How to Warn and Rebuke with Love

8. Before confronting another person's sin or error, the author says, "check your attitude," especially anger. List as many reasons as you can for why dealing with sin in anger makes problems worse and is ineffective in helping people.

Reflections

Don't rebuke or correct when you are angry. Wait until your anger is under control of the Holy Spirit (Gal. 5:15-23)....But when you are angry, recognize that uncontrolled anger inflames emotions, exaggerates issues, and hinders godly correction. It tends to be less rational and more self-justifying. It deals with people harshly. Loud, threatening talk can echo in a person's mind for a lifetime.

Leading with Love, page 143-144

The New Testament emphasizes treating people with gentleness, especially when correcting error or restoring a fallen believer. To be gentle with people is to be kind, tender, gracious, and calm—not harsh or combative. When confronting serious problems, Paul warns and corrects the Corinthians "by the meekness and gentleness of Christ" (2 Cor. 10:1).

Leading with Love, page 147

---

9. When correcting, rebuking, or disciplining a sinning brother or sister in Christ, what do the following passages of Scripture teach you about how this is to be done?

Galatians 6:1

2 Timothy 2:24-26

2 Timothy 4:2

2 Timothy 3:16, 17

10. If you needed to correct or rebuke a fellow believer who had displayed sinful outbursts of anger at home and at church, how would you use the Scriptures to effectively rebuke and at the same time help that person gain victory over a sinful temper? Lay out a plan you can use for helping such individuals in the future.

11. As a Christian leader, why is it imperative that you be gentle in spirit and conduct church discipline with gentleness?

The following verses will help you answer the question. Be aware that different translations may render the word *gentle* (Greek, *praÿtēs, praÿs* as *meekness, humility,* or *courtesy*):

Matthew 11:29-30; 2 Corinthians 10:1

1 Corinthians 4:21; Galatians 6:1

2 Timothy 2:25

Galatians 5:23; Ephesians 4:2; Colossians 3:12

1 Thessalonians 2:7; 2 Timothy 2:24 (Here the Greek word is *ēpios*, "gentle" or "kind.")

Reflections

**Love provides the right attitudes for exercising church discipline and
restoration. Love acts patiently and kindly; love is compassionate; it
feels for the misery of the impenitent sinner and seeks to relieve pain
and rescue from death. Loving hands are healing hands, both tender
and firm.**

Leading with Love, page 157

---

12. a. In practical terms, describe what dealing with people "in a spirit of
gentleness" (1 Cor. 4:21) would look like in practice.

b. Describe what the opposite of gentleness would look like in practice.

13. Explain the following verses and how they can help you deal more
effectively with people and their sins:

Proverbs 12:18b

Proverbs 16:24

Proverbs 18:21a

Proverbs 25:15b

Colossians 4:6

James 1:20

14. What practical steps can you take to be a more effective encourager of the people you lead? Share your ideas with others in your study group.

Reflections

Ultimately, then, refusal to confront a fellow believer's sin or false teaching in the name of tolerance and love is counterfeit tolerance and distorted love.... It was by the stern discipline imposed by Paul, not the church's lackadaisical tolerance, that the sinning member received genuine hope and help—that his "spirit may be saved in the day of the Lord" (1 Cor 5:5).

Leading with Love, page 163

Lesson Ten

The Works
of a Loving Leader

This lesson covers pages 165 to 184 of *Leading with Love*. Read these
pages before doing the lesson.

Begin Your Session by Reading the Passages Below

*But if you bite and devour one another, watch out that you are not
consumed by one another.* (Gal. 5:15)

*Above all, keep loving one another earnestly, since love covers a
multitude of sins.* (1 Peter 4:8)

*Beloved, never avenge yourselves, but leave it to the wrath of God,
for it is written, "Vengeance is mine, I will repay, says the Lord." To
the contrary, "if your enemy is hungry, feed him; if he is thirsty, give
him something to drink; for by so doing you will heap burning coals
on his head." Do not be overcome by evil, but overcome evil with
good.* (Rom. 12:19-21)

*For this is the love of God, that we keep his commandments. And
his commandments are not burdensome.* (1 John 5:3)

*If you keep my commandments, you will abide in my love, just as
I have kept my Father's commandments and abide in his love.*
(John 15:10)

Chapter 17: Managing Conflict a "More Excellent Way"

1. Examine and explain the meaning of Galatians 5:15.

Reflections

One of Satan's most successful strategies for keeping churches weak and ineffective is infighting and unresolved conflicts. This is a life-and-death issue in our local churches. So as a Christian leader, you will not have to face many conflicts, you will have to manage them according to biblical principles.

Leading with Love, pages 165-166

------

2. Below is a list of the fifteen descriptions of love (1 Cor. 13:4-7). Remember that each of the negative ones (the vices) has a positive counterpart. Use those also for answering questions.

Love According to 1 Corinthians 13:4-7

1. Patient
2. Kind

------

3. Not envious	Delights in the successes and talents of others
4. Not boastful	Promotes others
5. Not arrogant	Is humble and modest
6. Not rude	Displays proper decorum
7. Not selfish	Is self-sacrificing
8. Not easily angered	Calm
9. Not unforgiving	Forgives
10. Not joyful over wrongdoing	11. Rejoices with the truth

------

12. Bears all things
13. Believes all things
14. Hopes all things
15. Endures all things

a. Which two vices do you think are most responsible for creating conflict among Christians? Explain your answer.

b. Which two vices do you think are most responsible for perpetuating conflict and hindering resolution?

c. Which two virtues do you believe are most helpful in reducing conflict among believers? Explain your answer.

3. When you face conflict, and we all do, which two vices must you be most aware of in your personal life so that you don't accentuate and perpetuate the conflict?

———————————

Reflections

When their feelings have been hurt, people often feel justified in doing anything they want in retaliation. They can leave the church, divide the body, explode with uncontrolled anger, cut people off, lie, hate, and backbite. They try to justify the most wicked, sinful behavior with the simple excuse, "But I've been hurt!"

Leading with Love, page 172

———————————

4. The church at Philippi was experiencing internal conflict. Paul's overarching solution to such conflicts is given in Philippians 2:1-8:

> So if there is any encouragement in Christ, any comfort from love, any participation in the Spirit, any affection and sympathy, complete my joy by being of the same mind, having the same love, being in full accord and of one mind. Do nothing from rivalry or conceit, but in humility count others more significant than yourselves. Let each of you look not only to his own interests, but also to the interests of others. Have this mind among yourselves, which is yours in Christ Jesus, who, though he was in the form of God, did not count equality with God a thing to be grasped, but made himself nothing, taking the form of a servant, being born in the likeness of men. And being found in human form, he humbled himself by becoming obedient to the point of death, even death on a cross.

Explain how Philippians 2:1-8 helps reduce and temper conflict among believers.

5. Peacemaking is an act of love blessed by the Lord Jesus Christ.
   a. What are the character traits of loving, biblical peacemakers?

   b. In which areas of your life do you need to develop yourself as a loving, biblical peacemaker?

6. When Christians are engaged in bitter conflict, when harsh words have been exchanged and feelings have been deeply hurt, what does the Bible say a Christian's response is to be? List those responses with a Scripture reference for each. Be thorough in your answer.

7. In practical terms, how do you display love to people who dislike you or who you dislike because they have hurt your feelings?

Chapter 18: Obeying Christ's Commands and Teaching Others to Obey

8. In the section entitled, "Connecting Love and Leadership" (page 176), five examples are given of the connection between love and obedience. Summarize each of these points briefly in your own words. Which one of these points did you find most helpful to your own understanding of obedience and love? Explain.

9. a. What does the author mean when he says, "It's not enough to teach the facts about Christ, we are to teach, exhort, and train disciples to obey and live according to the commands of Christ"?

b. In what ways are you actively teaching and exhorting the people you lead to obey Christ's commands?

One of the greatest blessings a church can experience is for its leaders and teachers to love the Lord and delight in obeying his Word. It thrills the heart to see a church where the leaders are committed to obeying Scripture, eager to seek God's will, and determined to lead the church in ways that please the Lord. Such leaders are better leaders because they are far less inclined to neglect their God-given pastoral duties.

Leading with Love, page 183

10. Explain the following two passages of Scripture (1 Sam. 15:22-23): "Has the Lord as great delight in burnt offerings and sacrifices, as in obeying the voice of the Lord?"

"For rebellion is as the sin of divination."

11. The Old Testament Scriptures speak about Israelite kings who were half-hearted in their obedience to God. Give a modern-day example of half-hearted obedience to the Lord that results in serious harm to the local church.

12. In what ways are obedient leaders better leaders and teachers of the Lord's people and the church? List as many as you can.

13. What problems will you personally face if you merely hear about love and agree that love is important but don't daily practice the New Testament principle of love? Use James 1:22-26 to answer this question.

14. What practical steps can you take to become a more obedient practitioner of the New Testament principle of love?

Reflections

The Bible says, "Be doers of the word, and not hearers only, deceiving yourselves" (James 1:22). If we hear the words of God but do not obey them, we are self-deceived and his words have no lasting transforming power over us (James 1:22-25). Merely hearing God's words about love is not sufficient. We must set our minds on being eager "doers of the word."

Leading with Love, page 184

Other Titles from Lewis & Roth

**All of these titles can be ordered from
your local bookstore or through
Lewis & Roth Publishers
1.800.477.3239 ◆ www.lewisandroth.org**

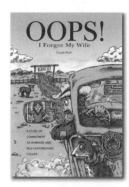

Oops! I Forgot My Wife offers a fresh and unique approach to encouraging healthy marriages. Communicating biblical truth through humor and story, author Doyle Roth challenges marriages to face their #1 enemy: self-centeredness, equips men for spiritual leadership in the home, provides a helpful resource for counseling and creates a user-friendly approach to evangelism.

> *Oops! I Forgot My Wife* (Hardback; 304 pages)
> *Oops! Discussion Guide* (Paperback; 48 pages)
> *Oops! Audio CD Set* (2 Audio CDs; 158 minutes)

Perhaps our greatest need as we train new generations of church leaders is for role models—godly examples of what loving Christian leadership should look like. Though largely unknown today, Robert Chapman (1803-1902) serves as just such an example. Featuring twelve "leadership lesson" snapshots drawn for Chapman's life, this inspiring little book demonstrates godly, pastoral leadership in action. Its short, easy-to-read chapters will challenge you to be a better leader, a more committed believer, and a brighter light to the world.

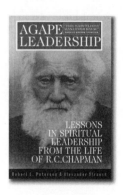

> *Agape Leadership* (Paperback; 76 pages)

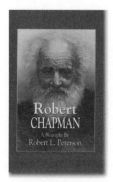

Charles Spurgeon once referred to Robert Chapman as "the saintliest man I ever knew." This full-length biography of Chapman tells the story of why he had such a marked impact on the lives of such men as George Muller, Hudson Taylor, Charles Spurgeon and others. It will challenge you to deepen your devotion to Christ and love others selflessly.

> *Robert Chapman: A Biography* (Hardback; 210 pages)

Hospitality may well be the best means we have to promote close, brotherly love. It is also an effective tool for evangelism. Showing Christ's love to others in a home environment may be the only means Christians have to reach their neighbors for Christ. Study questions and assignments for group discussion are included, making this an excellent resource for small groups and adult Sunday School classes.

The Hospitality Commands (Paperback; 68 pages)

With over 150,000 copies sold, this comprehensive book at the role and function of elders brings all the advantages of shared leadership into focus. Beginning with the four broad categories of eldering (leading, feeding, caring and protecting), *Biblical Eldership* explores the essential work of elders, their qualifications, their relationships with each other, and each of the biblical passages related to eldership. Written for those seeking a clear understanding of the mandate for biblical eldership, this book defines it accurately, practically and biblically.

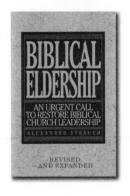

Biblical Eldership (Paperback; 340 pages)
Biblical Eldership Study Guide (Paperback; 176 pages)
Biblical Eldership Mentor's Guide (Paperback; 194 pages)

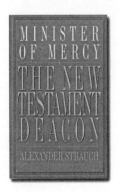

Deacons, as the New Testament teaches and as some of the sixteenth-century reformers discovered, are to be involved in a compassionate ministry of caring for the poor and needy. The deacons' ministry, therefore, is one that no Christ-centered church can afford to neglect. It's through the deacons' ministry that we make Christ's love a reality for many people. A groundbreaking study of all the biblical texts on the subject, *The New Testament Deacon* will help you build a strong ministry in your church.

The New Testament Deacon (Paperback; 192 pages)
The NT Deacon Study Guide (Paperback; 96 pages)